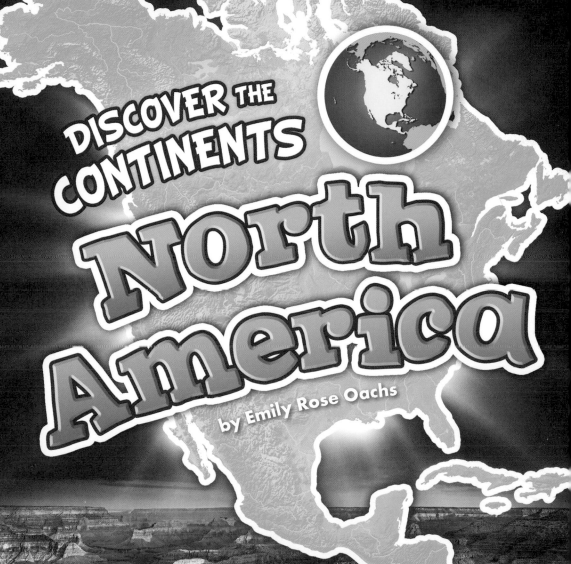

DISCOVER THE CONTINENTS

North America

by Emily Rose Oachs

BELLWETHER MEDIA • MINNEAPOLIS, MN

SHERWOOD BRANCH LIBRARY

Note to Librarians, Teachers, and Parents:

Blastoff! Readers are carefully developed by literacy experts and combine standards-based content with developmentally appropriate text.

Level 1 provides the most support through repetition of high-frequency words, light text, predictable sentence patterns, and strong visual support.

Level 2 offers early readers a bit more challenge through varied simple sentences, increased text load, and less repetition of high-frequency words.

Level 3 advances early-fluent readers toward fluency through increased text and concept load, less reliance on visuals, longer sentences, and more literary language.

Level 4 builds reading stamina by providing more text per page, increased use of punctuation, greater variation in sentence patterns, and increasingly challenging vocabulary.

Level 5 encourages children to move from "learning to read" to "reading to learn" by providing even more text, varied writing styles, and less familiar topics.

Whichever book is right for your reader, Blastoff! Readers are the perfect books to build confidence and encourage a love of reading that will last a lifetime!

This edition first published in 2016 by Bellwether Media, Inc.

No part of this publication may be reproduced in whole or in part without written permission of the publisher. For information regarding permission, write to Bellwether Media, Inc., Attention: Permissions Department, 5357 Penn Avenue South, Minneapolis, MN 55419.

Library of Congress Cataloging-in-Publication Data

Oachs, Emily Rose, author.
  North America / by Emily Rose Oachs.
    pages cm. – (Blastoff! Readers: Discover the Continents)
Includes bibliographical references and index.
  Summary: "Simple text and full-color photography introduce beginning readers to North America. Developed by literacy experts for students in kindergarten through third grade"– Provided by publisher.
  Audience: Grades K-3.
  ISBN 978-1-62617-328-6 (hardcover : alk. paper)
  1. North America–Juvenile literature. I. Title.
E38.5.O25 2016
970–dc23
                                      2015028684

Printed in the United States of America, North Mankato, MN.

Table of Contents

North America has rich land. The **continent** claims huge forests and other **natural resources**. Its farmland produces much of the world's food.

The Panama **Canal** is world famous. In the United States, people visit the Grand Canyon.

DID YOU KNOW?

○ The sun does not always set in the northernmost part of the continent during the summer.

○ A coast redwood in the United States is the world's tallest tree.

○ The Mississippi is one of the busiest rivers in the world!

coast redwood

Mississippi River

North America is in the Northern and Western **hemispheres**.

The Pacific Ocean lies to its west. The Arctic Ocean borders the north. To the east lie the Atlantic Ocean and Caribbean Sea. A strip of land connects North and South America.

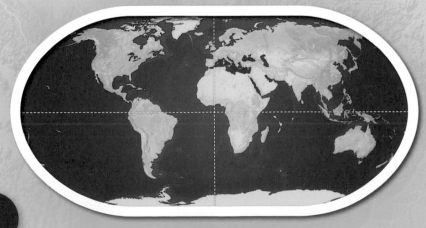

Arctic
Ocean

Atlantic
Ocean

Pacific
Ocean

Caribbean
Sea

South
America

N
W ✦ E
S

The Land and Climate

Rocky Mountains

The Rocky and Sierra Madre mountain ranges run through western North America. The Appalachian Mountains rise in the east. Low **plains** spread between the ranges.

The **Great Lakes** sit between Canada and the U.S. They hold much of the world's **freshwater**.

Great
Lakes

Rocky
Mountains

plains

Appalachian
Mountains

Sierra Madre
Mountains

Lake
Superior

N
W · E
S

Hot deserts lie in the U.S. and Mexico. Steamy **tropical rain forests** grow in **Central America**.

Sonoran Desert

Great Basin Desert

Sonoran Desert

Chihuahuan Desert

rain forest

rain forests

Mexico and Central America are warm all year. The northern U.S. and Canada are colder. These areas have warm summers and cold winters.

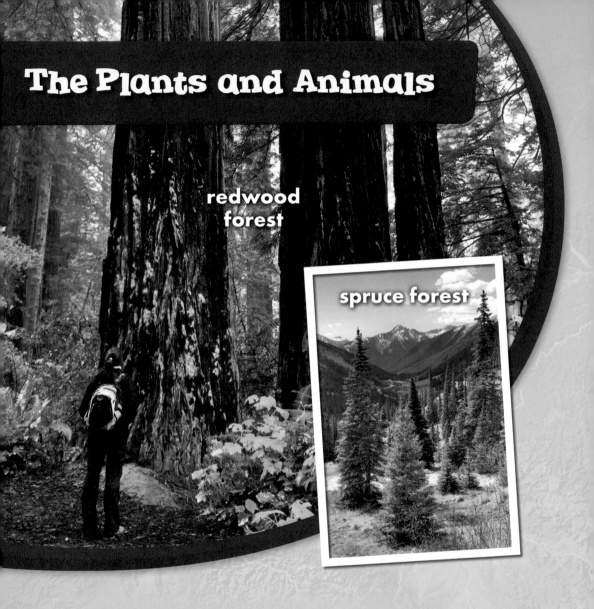

redwood
forest

spruce forest

Thick forests blanket the mountains. They circle the Great Lakes. In the west, spruce and redwood forests grow tall. Cactuses survive in dry deserts.

Orchids bloom in the rain forests.
Hibiscus flowers and spider lilies
grow on Caribbean islands.

hibiscus flower

spider
lilies

Green vine snakes and spider monkeys live in the rain forests. There, scarlet macaws fly between trees. In the north, polar bears swim in the ocean.

green vine snake

scarlet macaw

spider monkey

polar bear

monarch
butterflies

Monarch butterflies spend
summers in the U.S. and
Canada. Each fall, they
migrate to Mexico.

The People

Greenland
(Denmark territory)

United
States

Canada

N
W — E
S

United States

Dominican
Republic

Bahamas

Antigua
and
Barbuda

Haiti

Saint Kitts
and Nevis

Mexico

Cuba

Dominica

Barbados

Saint Vincent
and the
Grenadines

Belize

Jamaica

Grenada

Saint
Lucia

Honduras

Guatemala

Nicaragua

El Salvador

Panama

Trinidad
and
Tobago

Costa Rica

About 573 million people live
in North America. It has 23
different countries. Many are
Caribbean islands.

Mexico City is North America's largest city. Nearly 21 million people live there.

Mexico City

Mexico City

Aztec capital

The Spanish built Mexico City over an Aztec capital. The Aztecs were a powerful **native** group. They once ruled over much of Mexico.

Today, Mexico has native and Spanish **traditions**. North America mixes different **cultures** to form modern nations.

Fast Facts About North America

Size: 9.4 million square miles
(24.3 million square kilometers);
3rd largest continent

Number of Countries: 23

Largest Country: Canada

Smallest Country: St. Kitts and Nevis

Number of People: 573 million

Place with Most People: Mexico City, Mexico

Top Natural Resources: coal, oil, natural gas,
gold, iron, copper

Top Landmarks:
- Grand Canyon (United States)
- Statue of Liberty (United States)
- Panama Canal (Panama)
- Niagara Falls (United States and Canada)
- Chichén Itzá (Mexico)

Niagara Falls

Statue of Liberty

Grand Canyon

Canada

Chichén Itzá

Mexico City, Mexico

St. Kitts and Nevis

Panama Canal

N
W E
S

Glossary

canal—a waterway that is built to connect larger bodies of water

Central America—the narrow, southern part of North America

continent—one of the seven main land areas on Earth; the continents are Africa, Antarctica, Asia, Australia, Europe, North America, and South America.

cultures—the specific beliefs and practices of a group or region

freshwater—water that is not salty

Great Lakes—large freshwater lakes on the border between Canada and the United States

hemispheres—halves of the globe; the equator and prime meridian divide Earth into different hemispheres.

migrate—to travel from one place to another, often with the seasons

native—originally from a specific place

natural resources—materials in the earth that are taken out and used to make products or fuel

plains—large areas of flat land

traditions—customs, ideas, or beliefs passed down between families or cultures

tropical rain forests—thick, green forests that lie in the hot and wet regions near the equator

To Learn More

AT THE LIBRARY

Knudsen, Shannon. *Guatemala*. Minneapolis, Minn.:
Lerner Publications, 2011.

Marsh, Laura. *Great Migrations: Butterflies*.
Washington, D.C.: National Geographic, 2010.

Oxlade, Chris. *Introducing North America*. Chicago,
Ill.: Capstone Heinemann Library, 2014.

ON THE WEB

Learning more about
North America
is as easy as 1, 2, 3.

1. Go to www.factsurfer.com.

2. Enter "North America" into the search box.

3. Click the "Surf" button and you will see a
   list of related web sites.

With factsurfer.com, finding more
information is just a click away.

Index

The images in this book are reproduced through the courtesy of: prochasson frederic, front cover; tusharkoley, p. 4; Sergey Novikov, p. 5 (left); iofoto, p. 5 (right); kan_khampanya, p. 8; Kenneth Keifer, p. 9; Anton Foltin, p. 10; Francesco R. Iacomino, p. 11; Kris Wiktor, p. 12 (top); Alexey Kamenskiy, p. 12 (bottom); Bramwell Flora/ Alamy, p. 13 (top); FrankvandenBergh, p. 13 (bottom); Shaun Jeffers, p. 14 (left); NHPA/ SuperStock, p. 14 (top right); MNStudio, p. 14 (middle right); FloridaStock, p. 14 (bottom right); Lynnya, p. 15; ChameleonsEye, pp. 17, 19; traveler1116, p. 18 (top); National Geographic Creative/ Corbis, p. 18 (bottom); Christopher Gardiner, p. 21 (top left); Victor Maschek, p. 21 (top right); sumikophoto, p. 21 (middle); holbox, p. 21 (bottom left); Picturemakersllc, p. 21 (bottom right).